The Official
CHELSEA FC
Annual 2015

Written by David Antill, Richard Godden,
James Sugrue and Dominic Bliss

Thanks to Kevin Newman

Designed by Brian Thomson

A Grange Publication

© 2014. Published by Grange Communications Ltd., Edinburgh, under licence from Chelsea FC Merchandising Limited. www.chelseafc.com. Printed in the EU.

Photography ©Chelsea FC, Press Association, Action Images and Shutterstock

ISBN: 978-1-908925-64-0

£7.99

WELCOME

Welcome to The Official Chelsea FC Annual 2015!

It has been another exciting year for Chelsea, and we have all the best bits covered in this year's Annual. With José Mourinho now in his second season back at Stamford Bridge and some of the world's best players arriving at the club, Bridget and I have seen a lot of happy faces at Chelsea recently.

Of course, we even have a world champion in our squad now after André Schürrle's heroics during the World Cup in Brazil over the summer. You can read about all of that and plenty more in the pages to come.

Keep the blue flag flying high!

Stamford.

HONOURS LIST 2015

LEAGUE TITLES: FOUR
1955, 2005, 2006, 2010

FA CUPS: SEVEN
1970, 1997, 2000, 2007, 2009, 2010, 2012

LEAGUE CUPS: FOUR
1965, 1998, 2005, 2007

UEFA CHAMPIONS LEAGUES: ONE
2012

UEFA EUROPA LEAGUES: ONE
2013

EUROPEAN CUP WINNERS' CUPS: TWO
1971, 1998

UEFA SUPER CUPS: ONE
1998

COMMUNITY SHIELDS: FOUR
1955, 2000, 2005, 2009

FA YOUTH CUPS: FIVE
1960, 1961, 2010, 2012, 2014

CONTENTS

STORY OF THE SEASON

The 2013/14 season was full of ups and downs for the Blues – there is never a dull moment involving José Mourinho and Chelsea...

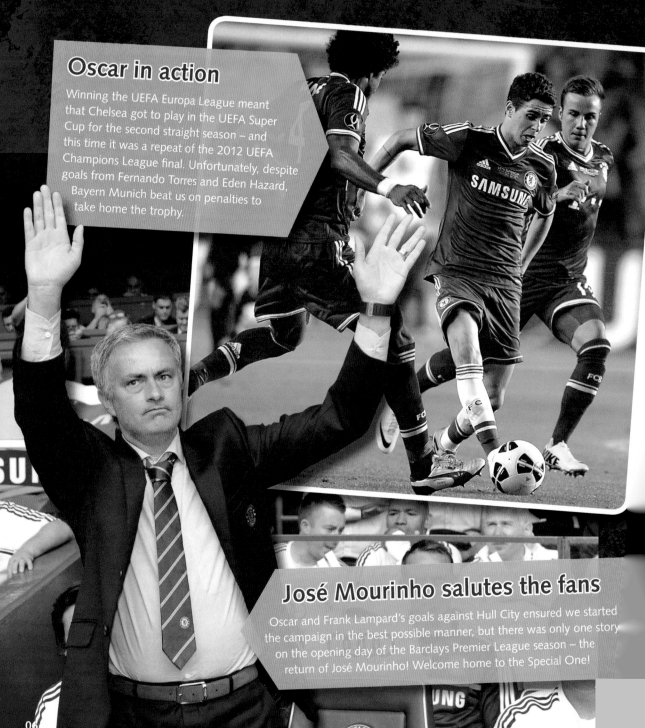

Oscar in action

Winning the UEFA Europa League meant that Chelsea got to play in the UEFA Super Cup for the second straight season – and this time it was a repeat of the 2012 UEFA Champions League final. Unfortunately, despite goals from Fernando Torres and Eden Hazard, Bayern Munich beat us on penalties to take home the trophy.

José Mourinho salutes the fans

Oscar and Frank Lampard's goals against Hull City ensured we started the campaign in the best possible manner, but there was only one story on the opening day of the Barclays Premier League season – the return of José Mourinho! Welcome home to the Special One!

Team-mates celebrate with

A collector's item at Stamford Bri
September – John Mikel Obi scori
The Nigerian had never previously
Premier League, but a superb vo
his account in the top flight aga
And didn't his team-mates enj

Willian v Norwich

Summer signing Willian gave Blues fans a
taste of things to come with a spectacular
strike against Norwich City to help the Blues
win at Carrow Road to put us third in the
Barclays Premier League standings.

es about to score anchester City

o Torres is about to take advantage
credible mix-up in the Manchester City
e to score the winning goal and send
rd Bridge wild. The Spanish striker
redator's instinct, striking the first
r Chelsea in the race for the Premier

Cahill scoring

Gary Cahill is more than just a centre-back –
he also chips in with his fair share of goals.
This unconventional effort against Southampton
helped the Blues recover from conceding in the first
minute to win the game 3-1, kicking December
off with a bang.

Hazard on fire!

Eden Hazard was in red-hot form in the thrilling 4-3
win over Sunderland. Gus Poyet, Black Cats manager
and a Blues legend, said of the Belgian: "I don't ever
remember a player playing against a side I have
managed as well as he did – no matter what we did
we couldn't cope with him."

Azpilicueta clears

The Blues kept Premier League top scorer Luis
Suarez and Liverpool quiet to record a 2-1 victory,
ensuring a successful Christmas period for the Blues.
Eden Hazard and Samuel Eto'o were the scorers
after we went behind early on, bringing 2013 to a
satisfactory conclusion.

Eto'o celebrates

Samuel Eto'o became the first player in al[l]
to score a hat-trick for Chelsea against Ma[n]
The Cameroonian scored for fun in games [at]
Bridge in 2013/14, but this treble was un[...]
highlight as he put the defending champ[...]
sword with a display of clinical finishin[g].

Ivanovic
scoring v C[ity]

Manchester City were [...]
unbeatable at the Etiha[d]
last season, but they we[re...]
for Chelsea! The Blues [...]
outplayed our title riva[ls...]
only surprise was that [...]
just one goal, scored b[y...]
Ivanovic, to show for a[...]
performance [...]

Hazard and Eto'o cel[...]

Eden Hazard must love playing clubs from the [...]
A great display against Sunderland in Decemb[er...]
followed up in February with a hat-trick aga[inst...]
United. One goal, which saw him link up wi[th...]
Eto'o, was out of this world – try to recreat[e...]
the playground!

Schürrle takes home the ball!

André Schürrle became the third Chelsea player to score a hat-trick – and take home the match ball – in 2014 with a superb treble against local rivals Fulham. Don't worry André, JT isn't trying to take the ball from you, he just wants to say well done!

Celebrating v Spurs

Another London derby: another comfortable Chelsea victory. This time it was Tottenham's turn to fall at the hands of the Blues, with Demba Ba scoring two late goals to seal a 4-0 win and ensure it's 24 years since Spurs won at the Bridge.

JT and Drogba

Didier Drogba, our UEFA Champions League hero in 2012, made an emotional return to Stamford Bridge with Galatasaray. Thankfully the players didn't let the tears distract them – a comfortable 2-0 win for the Blues saw us progress to the UEFA Champions League quarter-finals.

Oscar scoring

If you thought the 4-0 win against Spurs was as good as it gets, think again! Arsenal were thrashed 6-0 – that's right, six-nil – at the Bridge. What's more, it was Arsene Wenger's 1,000th game as Gunners boss! We lost track of the goalscorers because there were so many...

Champions League delight

Everyone thought Chelsea would be eliminated from the UEFA Champions League after a 3-1 first leg defeat against PSG – but the Blues don't give up without a fight and the French side were stunned by a thrilling comeback in the second leg. Even José Mourinho couldn't resist joining in the celebrations after Demba Ba scored!

Willian celebrates

Liverpool haven't won the league since 1990 and this run continued last season thanks to the Blues! Our 2-0 win late in the season, secured by goals from Demba Ba and Willian, was a major blow to the Reds. It's just a shame it wasn't enough for Chelsea to take the title, but there's always this season...

PLAYER

GOALKEEPERS

1 PETR CECH

Born: Plzen, Czech Republic, 20.05.1982   Height: 1.96m
Signed from: Rennes (July 2004)   Appearances: 478
Clean sheets: 220
Did You Know? Big Pete has kept more clean sheets for Chelsea than any other goalkeeper, surpassing Peter Bonetti's record last season. But he has some way to go to catch The Cat's tally of 729 appearances!

13 THIBAUT COURTOIS

Born: Bree, Belgium, 11.05.1992   Height: 1.99m
Signed from: Genk (July 2011)   Appearances: 0
Clean sheets: 0
Did You Know? Thibaut became the youngest-ever goalkeeper to represent the Belgian national side when he made his debut for the Red Devils against France in 2011.

23 MARK SCHWARZER

Born: Sydney, Australia, 06.10.1972   Height: 1.94m
Signed from: Free transfer (July 2013)   Appearances: 12
Clean sheets: 8
Did You Know? Last season saw Mark become the oldest player to represent Chelsea, as well as the oldest debutant in the history of the UEFA Champions League.

PROFILES

DEFENDERS

6 NATHAN AKE

Born: Gravenhage, Holland, 18.02.1995
Turned pro: July 2012
Goals: 0

Height: 1.80m
Appearances: 7

Did You Know? Nathan won Chelsea's Young Player of the Year award in 2013 and has been compared to Blues legend Ruud Gullit thanks to his dreadlocks!

28 CESAR AZPILICUETA

Born: Pamplona, Spain, 28.08.1989
Signed from: Marseille (August 2012)
Goals: 1

Height: 1.78m
Appearances: 92

Did You Know? After Chelsea's 4-0 win over Spurs last season, José Mourinho described Cesar – or Dave, as most fans call him – as "unbeatable"!

24 GARY CAHILL

Born: Sheffield, England, 19.12.1985
Signed from: Bolton Wanderers (January 2012)
Goals: 10

Height: 1.93m
Appearances: 111

Did You Know? Gaz's commanding displays in the 2013/14 campaign saw him earn a place in the PFA Team of the Year as voted for by professional footballers up and down the country.

2 BRANISLAV IVANOVIC

Born: Sremska Mitrovica, Serbia, 22.02.1984
Signed from: Lokomotiv Moscow (January 2008)
Goals: 25

Height: 1.85m
Appearances: 269

Did You Know? Branner scored in the last minute of the 2013 UEFA Europa League final to give Chelsea a 2-1 win over Benfica.

DEFENDERS (CONT)

3 FILIPE LUIS

Born: Santa Catarina, Brazil, 09.08.1985
Signed from: Atletico Madrid (July 2014)
Goals: 0

Height: 1.82m
Appearances: 0

Did You Know? Filipe learned how to speak English by watching Dirty Harry, starring Clint Eastwood, over and over again!

31 ANDREAS CHRISTENSEN

Born: Allerod, Denmark, 10.04.1996
Turned pro: July 2013
Goals: 0

Height: 1.88m
Appearances: 0

Did You Know? Andreas was in the starting line-up for both the Under-18s' FA Youth Cup final win and the Under-21s' Premier League play-off win over Manchester United.

26 JOHN TERRY

Born: Barking, England, 07.12.1980
Turned pro: March 1998
Goals: 57

Height: 1.87m
Appearances: 621

Did You Know? JT has worn the captain's armband for Chelsea an incredible 490 times, leading us to more silverware than any other skipper in the club's history!

5 KURT ZOUMA

Born: Lyon, France, 27.10.1994
Signed from: Saint-Etienne (January 2014)
Goals: 0

Height: 1.87m
Appearances: 0

Did You Know? Kurt grew up idolising John Terry – now he has the opportunity to partner the Blues skipper at the heart of Chelsea's defence.

PROFILES

MIDFIELDERS

4 CESC FABREGAS

Born: Arenys de Mar, Spain, 04.05.1987   Height: 1.80m
Signed from: Barcelona (June 2014)   Appearances: 0
Goals: 0
Did You Know? Cesc was just 16 years and 177 days old when he made his debut as a professional footballer for Arsenal in 2003.

10 EDEN HAZARD

Born: La Louvière, Belgium, 07.01.1991   Height: 1.73m
Signed from: Lille (July 2012)   Appearances: 111
Goals: 30
Did You Know? Eden was named PFA Young Player of the Year in 2014, adding to the equivalent award he twice won in France during his time with Lille.

21 NEMANJA MATIC

Born: Vrelo-Ub, Serbia, 01.08.1988   Height: 1.94m
Signed from: Benfica (January 2014)   Appearances: 22
Goals: 0
Did You Know? Nemanja is in his second spell with the Blues, having previously played for the club between 2009 and 2011.

12 JOHN MIKEL OBI

Born: Jos, Nigeria, 22.04.1987   Height: 1.88m
Signed from: Lyn Oslo (June 2006)   Appearances: 313
Goals: 4
Did You Know? Mikel doubled his tally of Chelsea goals last season by scoring twice, including his first-ever Barclays Premier League strike!

MIDFIELDERS (CONT)

8 OSCAR

Born: Americana, Brazil, 09.09.1991
Signed from: Internacional (July 2012)
Goals: 23
Height: 1.79m
Appearances: 111

Did You Know? Oscar made more tackles than any other player at the 2014 World Cup, which helped earn him a place in the Team of the Tournament.

7 RAMIRES

Born: Barra do Pirai, Brazil, 24.03.1987
Signed from: Benfica (August 2010)
Goals: 27
Height: 1.80m
Appearances: 196

Did You Know? Rammy is the only Brazilian to have scored in an FA Cup final, having opened the scoring against Liverpool in 2012.

17 MOHAMED SALAH

Born: Basuon, Egypt, 15.06.1992
Signed from: Basel (January 2014)
Goals: 2
Height: 1.75m
Appearances: 11

Did You Know? Mohamed scored three times against Chelsea for Basel in 2013 before being signed by the Blues!

14 ANDRE SCHURRLE

Born: Lugwigshafen, Germany, 06.11.1990
Signed from: Bayer Leverkusen (June 2013)
Goals: 9
Height: 1.83m
Appearances: 43

Did You Know? André became just the fourth player to lift the World Cup while representing Chelsea, following on from Peter Bonetti (England, 1966) and Frank Leboeuf and Marcel Desailly (France, 1998)

PROFILES

22 WILLIAN

Born: Ribeirão Pires, Brazil, 09.08.1988
Signed from: Anzhi Makhachkala (August 2013)
Goals: 4

Height: 1.75m
Appearances: 42

Did You Know? Before joining Chelsea, Willian played his part in helping Shakhtar Donetsk become the first Ukrainian team to win the UEFA Cup.

STRIKERS

19 DIEGO COSTA

Born: Lagarto, Brazil, 07.10.1988
Signed from: Atletico Madrid (July 2014)
Goals: 0

Height: 1.88m
Appearances: 0

Did You Know? Diego's 27 La Liga goals helped Atletico Madrid win the title for the first time since 1996!

11 DIDIER DROGBA

Born: Abidjan, Ivory Coast, 11.03.1978
Signed from: Galatasaray (July 2014)
Goals: 157

Height: 1.89m
Appearances: 341

Did You Know? Blues fans shouldn't need any reminder that it was Didier who slotted home the winning penalty in the 2012 UEFA Champions League final as we lifted the trophy for the first time.

18 LOIC REMY

Born: Rillieux-la-Pape, France, 02.01.1987
Signed from: QPR (August 2014)
Goals: 0

Height: 1.83m
Appearances: 0

Did You Know? Loic netted 14 Barclays Premier League goals for Newcastle United in the 2013/14 season.

All statistics correct to start of 2014/15 Barclays Premier League season.

JOSE MOURINHO

Go to Stamford Bridge on any given matchday and at some point you are likely to hear the Blues faithful singing the name of José Mourinho, who returned to Chelsea at the beginning of the 2013/14 season and announced that he was not just the club's manager, but a supporter too.

FIRST TIME AROUND...

In his first spell at the Bridge, between 2004 and 2007, Mourinho brought Chelsea our first league title for 50 years, and then repeated the feat the very next year. He also won the League Cup twice and led the club to glory in the first FA Cup final at the new Wembley.

It was a continuation of the success he had enjoyed in his previous job – his first major managerial post – at FC Porto, where he won the UEFA Cup and the UEFA Champions League in consecutive seasons, having also led them to back-to-back Portuguese league titles. It meant that, between 2002/03 and 2005/06, Mourinho won the league with his club four times, twice with Porto and twice with Chelsea. His success at Inter Milan and Real Madrid after he left Chelsea in 2007 ensured his place among the managerial greats in Italy and Spain as well, but now José is back in west London, where he truly feels at home.

THE SUCCESS STORY

CLUB HONOURS

Chelsea (2004-07)

Barclays Premier League (2005, 2006)

FA Cup (2007)

League Cup (2005, 2007)

FA Community Shield (2005)

Other Honours

UEFA Champions League (2004, 2010)

UEFA Cup (2003)

Primeira Liga (2003, 2004)

Portuguese Cup (2003)

Portuguese Super Cup (2003)

Serie A (2009, 2010)

Coppa Italia (2010)

Italian Super Cup (2008)

La Liga (2012)

Copa del Rey (2011)

Spanish Super Cup (2012)

BACK WHERE HE BELONGS

Upon his return to England in the summer of 2013, Mourinho talked about the things he had learned during his spells in Italy and Spain and how it could help him at Chelsea this time around.

"I learned a lot with these experiences: different players, different personalities, different cultures, different media, different structures in the club, but I think you still have to learn and improve every day.

"I want very much, more than ever, to do well. I want to do it because I am a professional and I want to do it because I am a supporter and this is the highest motivation I could feel in my career."

In his first season back at Stamford Bridge, Mourinho's Chelsea maintained a serious title challenge until the final weeks of the campaign and reached the UEFA Champions League semi-final. He now wants to go further in his quest to take the Blues back to the top in England and Europe.

INDIVIDUAL HONOURS

FIFA World Coach of the Year (2010)

UEFA Manager of the Year
(2003, 2004)

UEFA Team of the Year
(2003, 2004, 2005, 2010)

Barclays Premier League Manager of the Year
(2005, 2006)

Portuguese Primeira Liga Manager of the Year
(2003, 2004)

Italian Serie A Manager of the Year
(2009, 2010)

Miguel Munoz Trophy, Spain
(2011, 2012)

FAREWELL FRANK

I n the summer we said goodbye to Frank Lampard, one of the greatest players in Chelsea history, after 13 years of service at Stamford Bridge.

From the moment he signed in 2001 to the last game he played for the club, against Norwich in May 2014, he was a midfield marvel for the Blues, and a fans' favourite.

The part 'Super Frank' has played in our success over the past decade will never be forgotten...

CHELSEA'S ALL-TIME TOP SCORERS

With 211 goals to his name, Frank Lampard left Chelsea as the club's greatest-ever goalscorer. Here are the top 10 Blues scorers of all-time...

Frank Lampard 211

Bobby Tambling 202

Kerry Dixon 193

Didier Drogba 157*

Roy Bentley 150

Peter Osgood 150

Jimmy Greaves 132

George Mills 125

George Hilsdon 108

Barry Bridges 93

*watch this space!

UEFA Champions League winner: 2012

UEFA Europa League winner: 2013

Barclays Premier League winner: 2005, 2006, 2010

FA Cup winner: 2007, 2009, 2010, 2012

League Cup winner: 2005, 2007

FA Community Shield winner: 2005, 2009

CESC
FABREGAS

EDEN
HAZARD

WORLD CUP BLUES

There was a feast of football taking place in Brazil during the summer, as the South American nation hosted the World Cup for the first time since 1950. A record number of Chelsea players were taking part in these finals, with no less than 18 Blues stars named in their country's squads. Here are some of the best bits from an unforgettable tournament...

The 23-year-old breaks the deadlock with a cheeky finish in the second minute of extra-time during Germany's last-16 tie against Algeria.

Schürrle finds the back of the net with a sensational strike, scoring his second and Germany's seventh in their incredible 7-1 win over Brazil in the semi-finals.

Schürrle proudly lifts the FIFA World Cup trophy after helping Germany become the first European nation to win the competition in South America.

Blues winger André Schürrle celebrates with Mario Gotze after setting up the winning goal in extra-time of the final.

Blues legend Frank Lampard – who announced his departure from Chelsea just before the World Cup began – wore the captain's armband in England's final group game – a goalless draw with Costa Rica – on his 106th appearance for his country.

Eden Hazard meets Belgium's King Philippe and Queen Mathilde next to head coach Marc Wilmots at a royal reception after his country reached the quarter-finals of their first World Cup finals appearance since 2002.

Hazard and Blues 'keeper Thibaut Courtois line up for Belgium ahead of their quarter-final against Argentina. Can you spot any other familiar faces?

Young Chelsea defender Kenneth Omeruo stands firm against France's Olivier Giroud.

Cesar Azpilicueta looks in determined mood as he lines up for the Spanish.

Young Blues winger Christian Atsu gets to grips with Germany's Sami Khedira during Ghana's 2-2 draw with the eventual champions.

Our No.10 leaves an Algerian defender in his wake as he launches another attack.

Courtois spreads himself to deny Lionel Messi.

John Mikel Obi takes control in Nigeria's last-16 tie against France. The Blues midfielder featured in all four of his team's matches as they qualified from Group F along with Argentina.

Willian celebrates after his country secure a place in the quarter-finals.

The reigning champions may not have got out of their group, but Fernando Torres was on the scoresheet at a sixth major tournament for Spain, netting in their final group-stage game against Australia…

Oscar and Ramires celebrate as Brazil get off to a winning start. Oscar scored the third goal in a 3-1 win over Croatia in the tournament's opening game to send the home fans wild.

CECH'S CLEAN

Petr Cech showed he is one of the best goalkeepers around by winning the 2013/14 Barclays Premier League Golden Glove award. The prize is given to the 'keeper who has kept the most clean sheets at the end of the season, with Cech and Arsenal's Wojciech Szczesny taking the honour jointly, despite our No.1 playing three games fewer.

SHEET RECORD

"It's always nice to get recognition, and it's nice to have the most clean sheets from every goalkeeper," said Cech. "It's thanks to the way we played well defensively, but as a goalkeeper you need to be there to make sure you actually get the clean sheet. It's always nice to finish with something positive and the Golden Glove is a very positive thing."

Cech kept an impressive 16 clean sheets in 34 Premier League games in 2013/14. But that was still short of his own club record of 24 shut-outs in 35 appearances, set in 2004/05.

It's not the first time the Blues goalkeeper has proven his ability to stop the opposition scoring, as he also received the award in his first season in England, 2004/05, and again in 2009/10. That means this is the third time he has won the award, equalling the record held by Pepe Reina and Joe Hart.

It was the 32-year-old's second top-flight honour of the season, having already been named in the Professional Footballers' Association Team of the Season. He was one of three Chelsea players in that line-up, alongside Gary Cahill and Eden Hazard.

THE SELECTOR

Throughout the 2013/14 season Chelsea's first-team squad picked out their best, worst and first for a variety of subjects. Here are the highlights...

BEST GAME

RAMIRES: Every Chelsea supporter remembers this game. We were losing 2-0 against Barcelona in the Champions League semi-final in 2012 and then I managed to score a beautiful goal, which won the Goal of the Season award at the end of the season. There was a lot of pressure in the Camp Nou and we needed to be very focused. Of course, the person who scores gets the plaudits, but the whole team worked together to get that victory. In the end, together we managed to reach the final and win the Champions League.

WORST TV

ANDRE SCHURRLE: When people are in the jungle in Australia. What's it called? "I'm a Celebrity..." - we have the same in Germany and the British one was on before it, so I watched two weeks of the British one and two weeks of the German one, and I think this is really bad but it is funny.

ARDEST
OPPONENT

WILLIAN: Barcelona. Everybody knows their strengths and they have been one of, if not the, best team in recent years.

RST
PPONENT

AZPILICUETA: The
ugh opponent I came
inst when I played for
na was Roberto Carlos.
on after about 65
es to play on the right
o I was directly up
t him, when he was
g for Real Madrid. It
good experience, but
tunately we lost the
n 2-0.

BEST MUSIC

OSCAR: One of my favourites is "Every Breath You Take" by Sting and The Police. I have the tattoo of s of the lyrics around my arm, which is in memory of r father, who passed away.

FIRST HOLIDAY

EDEN HAZARD: My first holiday was to Spain. I can't remember exactly where, bu remember I went with my whole family; my cousins, my uncles and aunts, my br – there were about 40 of us! I have a big family. I think we played football every

FOREVER BLUE

Chelsea and adidas again came up with an eye-catching campaign to launch the 2014/15 home kit. The Forever Blue campaign featured five Blues players picking their favourite moments from their time at Stamford Bridge and helping adidas recreate it in a sculpture. The stunning launch video then saw the players breaking out from their sculptures to reveal the new kit, ready to make more amazing Chelsea moments.

PETR CECH v Bayern Munich, 19.05.12, 125mins 52 secs

Petr Cech dives across the TV studio to relive the moment he got a finger tip to Bastian Schweinsteiger's penalty in the 2012 UEFA Champions League final shootout. His touch saw the shot hit the post, setting up Chelsea's first-ever UEFA Champions League triumph.

OSCAR v Juventus, 19.09.12, 32mins 41secs

The crew use photos to help Oscar recreate the exact pose from his favourite moment, down to the smallest detail. The Brazilian chose hitting his wonder goal against Juventus in the 2012/13 UEFA Champions League group stage, when he knocked the ball past one defender before curling in a shot on the turn from outside the area.

EDEN HAZARD v Newcastle United, 08.02.14, 27mins 34secs

The adidas staff apply the liquid mould to Eden Hazard's face to make sure they get his likeness spot on. Hazard chose the most recent moment of any player, going for his first Chelsea hat-trick, scored against Newcastle at Stamford Bridge last season.

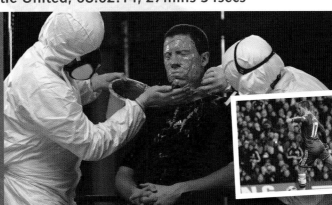

FERNANDO TORRES v Benfica, 15.05.13, 58mins 55secs

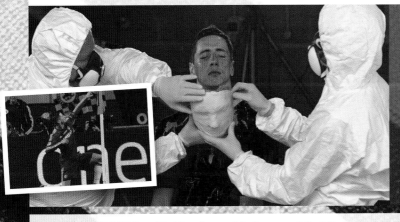

The finished mould of Fernando Torres's face is carefully removed from the Spaniard, ready to be turned into a sculpture of the striker soaking up the applause after scoring the opening goal in the 2013 UEFA Europa League final. Torres chose his celebration from that match in Amsterdam as his highlight with the Blues.

GARY CAHILL v Tottenham Hotspur, 20.10.12, 17mins 41secs

Gary Cahill bursts free from his sculpture. The defender chose to recreate his thunderous volley against Tottenham, when he opened the scoring in a 4-2 win at White Hart Lane in spectacular fashion.

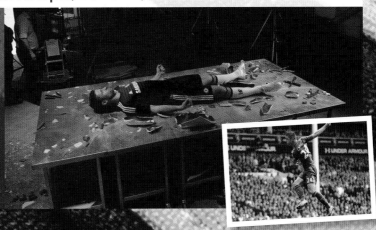

CHELSEA HISTORY: CHAMPIONS 2005

This season marks the tenth anniversary of the first of Chelsea's three Premier League title triumphs to date. A decade has passed since José Mourinho led a team with Petr Cech, John Terry, Claude Makelele, Frank Lampard and Didier Drogba at its spine to league glory and made Chelsea champions for the first time in 50 long years. We look back at a season for the ages...

HARD TO BEAT

The 2004/05 title-winning team was strong from the back to the front, and Chelsea's champions broke several records on their way to lifting the Barclays Premier League trophy, including the record for the meanest defence. With Petr Cech in goal, and four of Paulo Ferreira, John Terry, William Gallas, Ricardo Carvalho or Wayne Bridge making up the defence on most occasions, we conceded just 15 goals all season, losing only one game out of 38 in doing so.

THE SPECIAL ONE ARRIVES

José Mourinho took over the reins for the first time at Chelsea in the summer of 2004 and it took very little time before we realised we had a manager with the charisma to turn a very good team into a great one.

Only a year after arriving in London, the Portuguese manager had led his players to League Cup glory and, most importantly, to that long-awaited league title – all in his first season at the helm.

WONDER WINGERS

Chelsea also set the record for the most wins in a season, achieving 29 victories from the 38-game campaign, and having a frontline spearheaded by Didier Drogba or Eidur Gudjohnsen had a lot to do with that. However, they were supplied by some of the best wing play ever seen at Stamford Bridge, as Damien Duff, Arjen Robben and Joe Cole ran riot on the flanks. The rapid wide men gave defenders a torrid time all season and a fair few hammerings were dished out to hapless opponents.

A BIG DAY IN BOLTON

No team has ever won more away games than Chelsea did in 2004/05, as the Blues took all three points from 15 of their 19 matches on the road. The most memorable of those triumphs was the one that clinched the title at Bolton Wanderers' Reebok Stadium on 30 April, 2005.

A second-half double from Frank Lampard that day ensured that the title was sealed with three games to spare and the players celebrated, along with Roman Abramovich and the supporters in the away end, long after the final whistle. The Blues fans had waited a long time for that moment and victory tasted sweet!

They lifted the trophy after the next game at Stamford Bridge, a 1-0 win over Charlton sealed with a last-minute goal from Makelele who had never previously scored for Chelsea.

THE CHAMPIONS

Chelsea's squad in 2004/05 was one of the best the club has ever boasted. Here's how they weighed in over the course of that historic campaign:

PLAYER	APPEARANCES	GOALS
Frank Lampard	38	13
Eidur Gudjohnsen	30+7	12
John Terry	36	3
Claude Makelele	36	1
Petr Cech	35	0
Tiago	21+13	4
Damien Duff	28+2	6
Paulo Ferreira	29	0
William Gallas	28	2
Joe Cole	19+9	8
Didier Drogba	18+8	10
Ricardo Carvalho	22+3	1
Mateja Kezman	6+19	4
Arjen Robben	14+4	7
Glen Johnson	13+4	0
Alexey Smertin	11+5	0
Wayne Bridge	12+3	0
Jiri Jarosik	3+11	0
Geremi	6+7	0
Robert Huth	6+4	0
Celestine Babayaro	3+1	0
Scott Parker	1+3	0
Carlo Cudicini	3	0
Nuno Morais	0+2	0
Adrian Mutu	0+2	0
Lenny Pidgeley	0+1	0
Filipe Oliveira	0+1	0
Mikael Forssell	0+1	0
Anthony Grant	0+1	0
Steven Watt	0+1	0

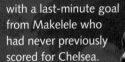

CHELSEA HISTORY:
CHAMPIONS 1955

Our first-ever league championship triumph!

It's not just in recent years that Chelsea have been lifting trophies. In fact, the 2014/15 season marks the 60th anniversary of our first-ever league championship triumph.

In the 1954/55 campaign, we won the old Division One – the equivalent of today's Premier League – under the management of former Arsenal and England forward Ted Drake. He had signed many of the players who would help us achieve our biggest success in the 50 years since the club was formed, with the likes of centre-back Peter Sillett and winger Frank Blunstone making a huge impact.

It wasn't just the squad that Drake changed, though. He was also responsible for a change in attitude at the club, making sure his players remained professional at all times and making us a team that other sides feared

By November 1954, nobody would have guessed that we'd win the league as we were positioned around the middle of the table. But with just four defeats in the final 26 games we managed to claim the title.

The most important match of the season came against Wolves at Stamford Bridge on Easter Saturday. They had beaten us 8-1 in an away game the year before, and more than 75,000 fans packed into the stadium to watch us try to get revenge.

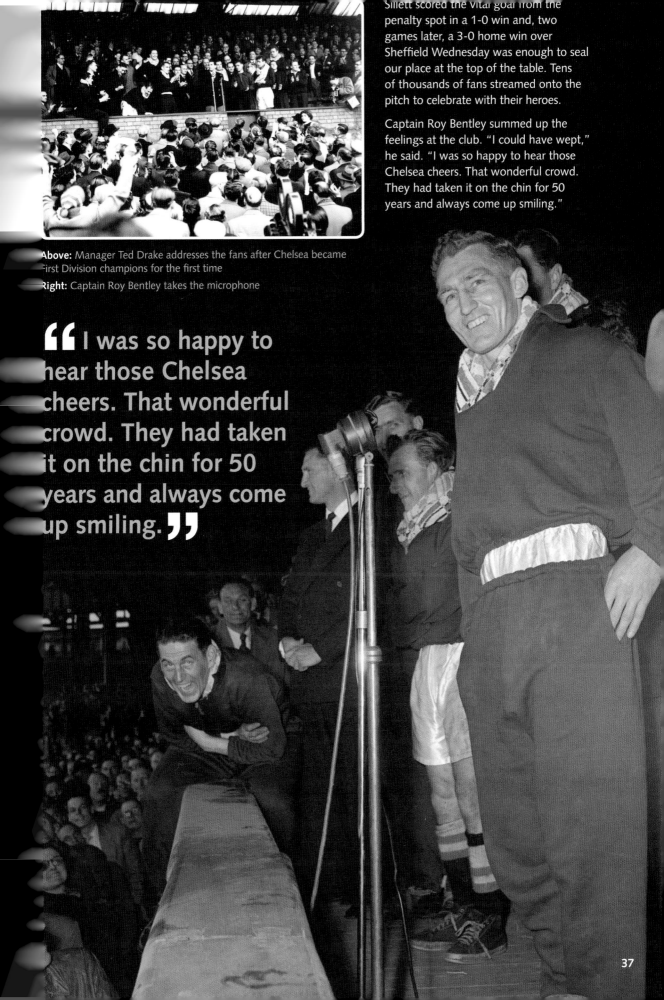

Sillett scored the vital goal from the penalty spot in a 1-0 win and, two games later, a 3-0 home win over Sheffield Wednesday was enough to seal our place at the top of the table. Tens of thousands of fans streamed onto the pitch to celebrate with their heroes.

Captain Roy Bentley summed up the feelings at the club. "I could have wept," he said. "I was so happy to hear those Chelsea cheers. That wonderful crowd. They had taken it on the chin for 50 years and always come up smiling."

Above: Manager Ted Drake addresses the fans after Chelsea became First Division champions for the first time

Right: Captain Roy Bentley takes the microphone

> **" I was so happy to hear those Chelsea cheers. That wonderful crowd. They had taken it on the chin for 50 years and always come up smiling. "**

SIDER: BEHIND THE SCENES ON THE SEASON

I love watching the Blues doing what they do best, winning football games. But what do the players get up to off the pitch? We take a look me of the behind-the-scenes highlights from the past year.

WILLIAN

Willian swaps places with the camera crew during a break in filming for a television advert for one of our partners. He seemed to enjoy the new role, although he was soon back in front of the camera to show off his football skills.

SALAH

Mohamed Salah, Marco van Ginkel, Nathan Ake and Ramires help this fan get a brilliant photo to remember her visit to our Cobham training ground. The players were definitely impressed when she showed them her special tool for taking the perfect selfie, meaning they were only too happy to get involved

CECH

Petr Cech attempts the Soccer AM crossbar challenge at Cobham as the rest of the Chelsea squad wait for their own turns. The players gave each other as much support as they could, but no-one managed the near-impossible trick of hitting the crossbar from the halfway line.

SCHURRLE

André Schürrle takes advantage of a temporary basketball hoop that was put up inside Stamford Bridge pitch for a visit by players from the Brooklyn Nets and Atlanta Hawks NBA teams. The German welcomed them to west London with a tour of the stadium before impressing with his own basketball talent.

DROGBA

Branislav Ivanovic and Didier Drogba catch up with a chat in the tunnel after our Champions League match against the striker's then club Galatasaray. We went on to beat the Turkish team over the two legs, but there clearly weren't any hard feelings between the former team-mates.

SPOT THE BALL

Can you work out which is the real ball in the picture below?

WORDSEARCH

Chelsea won our first top-flight league title in half a century 10 years ago, when José Mourinho led us to Premier League glory in 2004/05. The names of all 20 players who made 10 or more league appearances that season are hidden in the grid below. Can you find them all?

```
N  E  S  N  H  O  J  J  D  U  G  L  G  O  J
N  C  E  C  H  K  M  X  D  Y  P  V  G  O  O
T  N  L  F  H  J  A  R  O  S  I  K  A  H
I  J  L  Z  Z  G  A  H  J  Z  W  F  I  N
M  J  Q  T  D  P  L  M  S  Y  N  R  T  S
E  V  H  U  M  A  E  A  K  A  R  Y  F  O
R  R  F  A  V  L  G  K  D  E  L  R  Z  N
E  F  L  R  V  R  D  E  R  Z  Z  L  E  F
G  B  A  C  O  X  I  L  O  M  Z  M  A  T
L  C  Q  B  O  B  R  E  G  X  V  C  A  G
F  Z  B  H  N  L  B  L  B  D  V  P  W  N
X  E  T  G  Y  Q  E  E  A  Z  H  N  F  V
N  U  K  R  W  A  R  I  E  R  R  E  F  D
H  Q  B  N  I  T  R  E  M  S  Y  F  L  G
```

BRIDGE	DUFF	HUTH	MAKELELE
CARVALHO	FERREIRA	JAROSIK	ROBBEN
CECH	GALLAS	JOHNSON	SMERTIN
COLE	GEREMI	KEZMAN	TERRY
DROGBA	GUDJOHNSEN	LAMPARD	TIAGO

Answers on page 61

Chelsea's Under-21s celebrate their trophy triumph at the end of last season.

Chelsea Academy

The Chelsea Academy went into the 2014/15 season as holders of both the FA Youth Cup and the Barclays Under-21 Premier League after a year of glory...

UNDER-21s: PLAY-OFFS, PENALTIES AND PRAISE

In the Barclays Under-21 Premier League, finishing top of the league is not enough to take the trophy – you also have to triumph in the play-offs, and last

At the end of the league season, the top four teams in the table go into a play-off semi-final stage, with the winners meeting in a one-off final to determine the overall champions.

The Blues' Under-21s team had been in sensational form all season as they won the league, but they then faced a tricky game against fourth-place Manchester City in the play-offs semi-final.

In fact, after a 1-1 draw, the game went to penalties, but Chelsea's young goalkeeper Jamal Blackman was the star on the night, saving two of City's spot kicks as the Blues held their nerve to progress to a final with Manchester United at Old Trafford.

Away from home, but full of confidence, Chelsea won the final in normal time and then celebrated on the pitch like true champions. Goals from skilful winger Charly Musonda and the club's Young Player of the Year, captain Lewis Baker, secured the trophy

THE FA YOUTH CUP FINAL WINNERS 2014

Chelsea's Under-18s celebrate their third FA Youth Cup success since 2010.

UNDER-18s: STAMFORD BRIDGE GOES YOUTH CUP CRAZY

Chelsea have been the team to beat in the FA Youth Cup for many years now and last season we reached the final for the fourth time in five years, and won it for the third time since 2010.

This year we had to play our neighbours, Fulham, home and away in the final and it turned out to be a classic, ending 7-6 to Chelsea on aggregate!

Fulham won the first leg 3-2 at Craven Cottage, and they were 3-2 up at half-time in the second leg at Stamford Bridge too. Chelsea had to produce something special in the second half to come back, and we did just that.

Three goals in the last 15 minutes of the game – including a late equaliser and an even later winner from striker Dominic Solanke – had the crowd on their feet and the scenes of jubilation on the pitch after the game showed everyone just how much the victory meant to the club.

Lewis Baker celebrates the winning goal in the Barclays Under-21 Premier League play-off final.

43

WHERE AT STAMFORD BRIDGE ARE WE?

Take a trip around the home of the Blues and see if you can work out where these pictures were taken.

Answers on page 61

1

2

3

11-A-SIDE

How well do you know your favourite Chelsea stars?
Below are the names of 11 players and 11 Blues facts.
Can you match the facts to the correct players?

PLAYERS

1 Petr Cech

2 Branislav Ivanovic

4 Cesc Fàbregas

7 Ramires

10 Eden Hazard

11 Oscar

14 André Schürrle

15 Mohamed Salah

21 Nemanja Matic

24 Gary Cahill

26 John Terry

FACTS

A My injury-time header was the winning goal in the 2013 UEFA Europa League final.

B I scored the first hat-trick of my career for the German national team in October 2013, before scoring my first Chelsea hat-trick against Fulham in the same season.

C I am in my second spell with Chelsea, having left to play for Benfica for three years between 2011 and 2014.

D I was Chelsea's first new signing of the 2014 summer transfer window, moving to Stamford Bridge from Barcelona.

E I have won the Czech Republic's Footballer of the Year award a record seven times.

F I won the UEFA Champions League and FA Cup in my first season after joining Chelsea from Bolton Wanderers in January 2012.

G I scored in two games against Chelsea in last season's UEFA Champions League before moving to Stamford Bridge in January.

H I graduated from the Chelsea youth Academy and have gone on to become the club's most successful captain of all time, winning 13 trophies as skipper.

I I wore the No.17 shirt in my first two years with Chelsea, but changed to the No.10 for this season.

J I was nicknamed the "Blue Kenyan" because of my running and stamina while playing in my homeland Brazil.

K I won Chelsea's Goal of the Season award in 2012/13 for one of the two goals I scored against Juventus on my first start for the Blues.

Answers on page 61

COMPETITION
WIN A SIGNED CHELSEA SHIRT!

Answer the following question correctly and you could win a Chelsea shirt signed by a first-team player.

In what season did Chelsea start wearing an adidas kit?

A) 1986/87
B) 1996/97
C) 2006/07

Entry is by email only. Only one entry per contestant. Please enter **CFC SHIRT** followed by either **A**, **B** or **C** in the subject line of an email. In the body of the email, please include your full name, address, postcode, email address, phone number and date of birth and send to: frontdesk@grangecommunications.co.uk by Friday 27th March 2015.

JOIN IN
JUNIOR

TRUE BLUE MEMBERSHIP

ONLY £15

PLAYER OF THE YEAR 2014

Fans' favourite Eden Hazard won the club's Player of the Year award for the 2013/14 campaign. The Belgian winger wowed supporters with his silky skills, mazy dribbles and stunning goals and it was no surprise to see him walk away with the main prize, which was presented to him by José Mourinho.

"I just want to say thank you, thank you to all of you," was his message to the supporters. "We know it's a collective sport but individually trophies are sometimes good, so I'll take this one home and enjoy it with my family."

Hazard was also named PFA Young Player of the Year, as well as being voted for the senior version of that award. The Belgian winger was one of three Blues players to be named in the PFA Team of the Year, along with Petr Cech and Gary Cahill.

DID YOU KNOW?

As well as scoring 17 goals last season, Eden Hazard also set up 13. In his first two seasons with the Blues, he made 111 appearances!

Hazard was also named PFA Young Player of the Year

Lewis Baker won Young Player of the Year and Goal of the Season

BRIGHT YOUNG THING

Talented Academy midfielder Lewis Baker had two reasons to celebrate when he was named Young Player of the Year as well as winning Goal of the Season for his amazing mid-air back-heel volley against Arsenal Under-21s. Three days later he had another trophy in his hands after our Under-21s beat Manchester United to win the Barclays Under-21 Premier League play-off. To top it all off he scored the winning goal in that 2-1 victory.

TEAM PLAYER

Cesar Azpilicueta made himself one of the most important members of the Chelsea squad last season and his team-mates clearly appreciated his efforts when they named him Players' Player of the Year. Azpi – or Dave as some of the Blues fans call him – made the left-back spot his own. Pretty good going when he had played at right-back before that and the man he replaced, Ashley Cole, is one of the greatest defenders this country has ever produced and a true Blues legend.

Cesar Azpilicueta talks to co-host Gigi Salmon after winning Players' Player of the Year

Paulo Ferreira receives his award from Sebastian Coe

PRIZE FOR PAULO

The 2014 Special Recognition award went to a man who played as a full-back not too long before Azpilicueta and he received a great reception from fans at the event. Paulo Ferreira was signed by José Mourinho during his first spell at the club and spent nine years with the Blues. He won ten major honours here, including three Premier Leagues, the UEFA Champions League and UEFA Europa League. After leaving the club in 2013, Paulo is now taking his coaching badges.

SIZZLING STRIKES

GOALS OF THE SEASON

Chelsea scored exactly 100 goals in all competitions during the 2013/14 season. There were plenty of belters among them, so we look back at some of the best Blues strikes that got the fans off their seats...

WILLIAN

v Norwich City, Carrow Road,
Barclays Premier League,
06.10.13

With 10 minutes left, the Chelsea fans got a first look at our new signing Willian, when the Brazilian midfielder came on as a substitute for Juan Mata. It didn't take Willian long to make a spectacular introduction. The ball broke loose in the corner of the penalty area and our No.22 coolly curled a shot around goalkeeper John Ruddy.

EDEN HAZARD

v Newcastle United,
Stamford Bridge,
Barclays Premier League, 08.02.14

Hazard scored his first hat-trick for Chelsea to give us a 3-0 win, but it was his second goal that stood out. The Belgian cut in from the left wing and rolled the ball to Samuel Eto'o. Our No.29 played an outrageous back-heel flick that surprised everyone, apart from Hazard, who had continued his run to slot the ball into the back of the net.

FERNANDO TORRES

v Bayern Munich, Eden Arena (Prague), UEFA Super Cup, 30.08.13

The Spanish striker finished off a brilliant team move by thundering his first-time shot in off the right post, but the real beauty was in the build-up. Eden Hazard left two defenders stumbling to the ground and slid a pass to André Schürrle, whose low ball into the box found Torres perfectly.

ANDRE SCHURRLE

v Stoke City, Britannia Stadium, Barclays Premier League, 07.12.13

When Schürrle got the ball from John Mikel Obi he took on the whole Stoke defence single-handed. Ryan Shawcross was left dizzy after being turned left, then right, then left again before our German winger found the bottom corner from the edge of the area.

SAMUEL ETO'O

v Arsenal, Stamford Bridge, Barclays Premier League, 22.03.14

Our amazing 6-0 win over the Gunners started in style when Eto'o scored after just two minutes. The Cameroon captain got the ball on the right of the penalty area with two defenders blocking his way to the goal, but he sent them both the wrong way before curling a shot past goalkeeper Wojciech Szczesny.

NAME THE SCORER...

Can you guess who scored these goals and who against last season from the pictures and the clues?

GOAL 1

We scored a record number of goals against these opponents in this game.

This was the final goal of the game.

It was against one of our London rivals.

The scorer signed for us in January 2014.

GOAL 2

This game saw a Chelsea legend play at Stamford Bridge again for the first time since leaving.

Samuel Eto'o scored the other goal in this game.

The scorer is a defender who won the UEFA Champions League with Chelsea.

TRUE OR FALSE?

1 Chelsea had two players in the PFA Team of the Year last season.

2 Last season Frank Lampard became the only Chelsea player to earn 100 international caps while playing for the club.

3 Chelsea's pitch was dug up in the summer and donated to Aldershot Town FC.

4 Chelsea were originally nicknamed The Pensioners.

5 Stamford Bridge used to have a horse-racing track around the outside of the playing surface.

WHO ARE WE?

They played for the Blues before you were even born, but can you name these two legends?

Answers on page 61

Eden Hazard helps launch the club's Asian Star initiative for 2014

John Terry and Didier Drogba leave the field after our 2-0 win over Drogba's then club Galatasaray in the UEFA Champions League

PICTURE PERFECT

CHECK OUT A SELECTION OF OUR FAVOURITE IMAGES FROM THE 2013/14 SEASON, TAKEN FROM THE CLUB'S OFFICIAL INSTAGRAM PAGE!

More joy for the Chelsea Academy after we won the Barclay's Under-21 Play-off final

Frank Lampard receives a special trophy to mark his 100th cap for England

John Mikel Obi celebrates his goal against Fulham – his first for Chelsea since January 2007

Demba Ba is congratulated by Oscar after scoring his second goal in our 4-0 win over Tottenham

Brooklyn Nets basketball star and Chelsea fan Kevin Garnett sits in the dug-out during a visit to Stamford Bridge

Oscar poses with his sculpture, which was produced as part of the adidas Forever Blue campaign to launch the new home kit

Dominic Solanke celebrates scoring the winning goal in the FA Youth Cup final...

The teams are led out by Chelsea Pensioners ahead of our game against West Brom to mark Remembrance Day

... and the players celebrate in the dressing room afterwards

CHELSEA LADIES

Chelsea Ladies are one of the top teams in the FA Women's Super League, with a squad packed full of quality players – including a World Cup winner. Meet the girls who wear the Blue shirt with pride...

STAR PLAYERS

KATIE CHAPMAN AND GILLY FLAHERTY

The Blues pulled off a huge transfer coup ahead of the start of last season by signing two of Arsenal's best players, Gilly Flaherty (above, right) and Katie Chapman (above, left)!

YUKI OGIMI

Yuki Ogimi (below) arrived at Chelsea as a UEFA Champions League and World Cup winner! The Japanese striker is a superstar in her homeland!

JI SO-YUN

Ji So-Yun (above) scored against Chelsea in the International Women's Club Championship in 2013 – and then signed for the Blues! Emma Hayes reckons she plays like Lionel Messi.

LAURA BASSETT AND RACHEL WILLIAMS

Chelsea Ladies fans had bad memories of Laura Bassett (below, left) and Rachel Williams (below, right) before the duo signed for us – they were part of the Birmingham side which beat the Blues in the 2012 FA Women's Cup final.

DID YOU KNOW?

JACKIE GROENEN (below) isn't just a great footballer – she also has a Judo black belt.

CHELSEA LADIES travelled to Japan to take part in the International Women's Club Championship. The squad may have lost in the final to INAC, who are from Japan, but it was a great experience and the Blues did the club proud.

EMMA HAYES (below) is the Chelsea Ladies manager and she has experienced "soccer" in the USA, as well as being a coach at Arsenal when the Gunners became the first English side to win the Women's UEFA Champions League.

Keep up to date with the Chelsea Ladies via their Twitter page, @ChelseaLFC.

CHELSEA FC
SOCCER SCHOOLS

BOYS & GIRLS OF ALL ABILITIES AGED 4-13 YEARS

COURSES INCLUDE: MINI KICKERS, ADVANCED & GOALKEEPERS

Operating in the following areas during every holiday period:

Surrey, Berkshire, Middlesex, London, Essex, Hampshire, Wiltshire, Sussex & Kent

Visit **chelseafc.com/foundation** for your nearest venue

SAVE 10% WHEN YOU BOOK ONLINE

QUIZ ANSWERS

Page 40

Spot the Ball

Page 41

Wordsearch

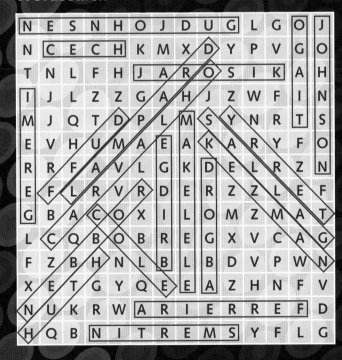

Page 44

Where In Stamford Bridge Are We?

1   Press room
2   Peter Osgood statue
3   The original "Shed" wall
4   Home dressing room
5   Chelsea Museum
6   Players' tunnel
7   The Megastore
8   Box office

Page 46

11-a-Side

Petr Cech – E
Branislav Ivanovic – A
Cesc Fàbregas – D
Ramires – J
Eden Hazard – I
Oscar – K
André Schürrle – B
Mohamed Salah – G
Nemanja Matic – C
Gary Cahill – F
John Terry – H

Page 55

Name the Scorer...

Goal 1: Mohammed Salah v Arsenal
Goal 2: Gary Cahill v Galatasaray

True or False?

1   False – we had three (Eden Hazard, Petr Cech and Gary Cahill)
2   True
3   True
4   True
5   False – it was a greyhound track

Who Are We?

Ron Harris and Peter Bonetti

WHERE'S STAMFORD?

Can you find Stamford hiding in the crowd? And did you spot Bridget hiding on an earlier page in the Annual?